Dying to Tell You

A record of personal details and end of life planner

Kathryn Perks

CONTENTS

Foreword

During our lifetime we seldom consider preparing for our death or what will happen to our possessions when that time comes, or more importantly who might be given the unenviable task of trying to make sense of all that we leave behind. Often our siblings or children live in different cities or countries and we put off discussing with them what we know we should. It just never seems to be the right time and for some of us it can be a sensitive topic to raise, even with those closest to us. It is however usually our family members who are faced with this responsibility and are expected to step in.

When my mother died our family were relieved that she had at least collated her important documents, but she had left us no guidelines regarding her funeral service. Luckily, we were all in agreement when it came to selecting hymns and readings, but what if we hadn't been? We made funeral arrangements and hoped our choices were what she would have wanted, but how could we be sure? She had told us her preference regarding burial or cremation so we didn't have to make that decision and she had prepared a Will, but we anguished over why we had not discussed with her all that was suddenly unknown and how that would have helped us decide what to do.

At that time, I was living overseas and had taken leave from my job. There was a house full of her possessions to sort through so that it could be put up for sale. As none of the family lived close by, this all had to be done as a matter of urgency. I started going through her papers, hoping everything was in order but it soon became clear that this was going to be a challenging and lengthy task. In fact, it was overwhelming. Was what she had kept still relevant and current? I discovered that some companies had changed their names and some no longer existed. What could I throw out with any certainty, and where on earth should I start? All this was at a time when I was in a state of grief. Administrative concerns were the last thing on my mind. I just wanted someone to step in and take the burden away.

It was then I started thinking about how I might make it easier for whoever has to sort through my own accumulation of 'stuff' when I die. What would be helpful? I thought that by creating a readily accessible point of reference which contains my personal details, this would surely help reduce some of the stress for whoever gets this job. I passed the idea around friends and family who were all encouraging, and those I spoke to who had lost parents said how they wished there had been something similar available to them so they may have been more sure their choices were what their loved ones would have wanted.

Dying to Tell You was created as an aid, initially for myself, to help record my important information in one place. I hope that you will also find it useful and that it may prompt you to consider, share and discuss your wishes with your family or friends, so that the administration of your estate will be an easier process for them.

Guide to Completion

This booklet is not intended to replace your Will. It is a tool in which to record all the 'extra' bits that may not be recorded in your Will and to assist with the administration of your estate. I hope that your family will respect and follow your requests, however your lawyer should be consulted.

It may seem an overwhelming task, and it does require your application, but pick away at it and when completed it will be a useful source of information. Tick only those boxes that apply to your choices, or if space is provided complete in legible handwriting, taking care that contact details in particular are accurately and clearly recorded.

Where should I keep this?

Remember the booklet needs to be readily accessible. On completion you may wish to copy some pages for your lawyer, but it's a good idea to keep it with all your personal documents in one safe place. Examples of your documents might include passport, certificates (birth, citizenship, marriage, divorce) business contract, property rates notice or valuation certificate, car registration, Trust details, correspondence from banks, insurance policies or any other documentation from individuals or organisations that you record details of within this booklet.

Who should I tell?

It is vital that you let your family members or friends know that you have completed this booklet, and its location. **I also recommend that you advise your lawyer about its existence upon completion.**

REVIEWS / UPDATES

Reviews of all entries should be made regularly so the contents are always up to date. If your selections change after initial completion, record these as soon as possible (refer to page 37).

Information reviewed and last updated on:

_______________	_______________	_______________	_______________
(Date)	(Your signature)	(Date)	(Your signature)
_______________	_______________	_______________	_______________
(Date)	(Your signature)	(Date)	(Your signature)
_______________	_______________	_______________	_______________
(Date)	(Your signature)	(Date)	(Your signature)
_______________	_______________	_______________	_______________
(Date)	(Your signature)	(Date)	(Your signature)
_______________	_______________	_______________	_______________
(Date)	(Your signature)	(Date)	(Your signature)
_______________	_______________	_______________	_______________
(Date)	(Your signature)	(Date)	(Your signature)
_______________	_______________	_______________	_______________
(Date)	(Your signature)	(Date)	(Your signature)
_______________	_______________	_______________	_______________
(Date)	(Your signature)	(Date)	(Your signature)
_______________	_______________	_______________	_______________
(Date)	(Your signature)	(Date)	(Your signature)

PERSONAL PRIORITISED INFORMATION

SURNAME: _______________________ **Given names:** _______________________

Previous surnames / previously known as: _______________________

Address: _______________________ **Country:** _______________________

Date of birth: _______________________ **Place of birth:** _______________________

I am a Justice of the Peace: Yes ☐   No ☐

Nationality: *(where legally a citizen)* _______________________

If not born in the country where you currently reside, when did you arrive? _______________________

Marital status: Married ☐   De facto ☐   Divorced ☐   Widowed ☐   Single ☐

Where married *(city/country):* _______________________ **Date married:** _______________________

Full name of spouse/partner *(at birth):* _______________________

Phone *(spouse):* _______________________ **Date of birth** *(spouse):* _______________________

Mother's full <u>maiden</u> name: _______________________

Occupation: _______________________

Father's full name: _______________________

Occupation: _______________________

<u>**FUNERAL**</u> *(see also page 13)*: I have a Funeral Fund or Prepaid Funeral Plan: Yes ☐   No ☐

<u>**DISPOSAL OF BODY:**</u> I wish to be cremated ☐   **Or:** I wish to be buried: ☐

<u>**LAWYER'S NAME:**</u> _______________________ Company: _______________________

Address: _______________________ Phone: _______________________

<u>**EXECUTOR**</u> I have appointed an Executor *(also refer to page 17)*:   No ☐   Yes ☐

Please contact the following person/s for Executor's details *(e.g. Lawyer)*: _______________________

_______________________ Phone: _______________________

<u>**WILL:**</u> I do <u>not</u> have a Will ☐   I have a Will ☐   a copy of which is held with:

Name *(e.g. of Lawyer)*: _______________________ Company: _______________________

Address: _______________________ Phone: _______________________

Or: I have prepared a Will myself *(e.g. publication purchased from newsagent)* ☐ and it is located:

____

MY WILL WAS LAST UPDATED ON: _______________ / _______________

_______________ / _______________

<u>**DOCTOR:**</u>

Doctor's Name: ________________________________ Medical Practice: ________________________________

Address: ____ Phone: ________________________________

<u>**LIVING WILL and/or ADVANCE CARE PLAN**</u> (ACP)

(A Living Will or Advance Care Plan outlines your instructions as to what you wish to happen in the event of you being unable to make or communicate decisions regarding your health care, e.g. If you become incapacitated through accident or illness):

I do **NOT** have a Living Will ☐   I do **NOT** have an Advance Care Plan ☐

I have a Living Will ☐   I have an Advance Life Care Plan ☐

My doctor has been made aware of my ACP ☐   My ACP is attached to my hospital medical file ☐

Contact details of who holds this documentation *(e.g. your Lawyer, Doctor etc)*:

Name / Organisation: ____

____ Phone: ________________________________

<u>**POWERS OF ATTORNEY:**</u> *The appointment of someone to make decisions or act on your behalf.*

(Note: Power of Attorney nominations cease to be effective upon death, however in the event of, for example, your mental incapacitation, it may be helpful to record the following information. Any such appointments should be made via your Lawyer).

I have nominated an Enduring Power of Attorney for my personal care and welfare ☐

I have nominated an Enduring Power of Attorney for my property ☐

Contact details of who holds this documentation, *e.g. your Lawyer:*

Name: ________________________________ Company:________________________________

Phone: ________________________________

<u>**TRUSTS:**</u>

I have set up a Trust: <u>Type</u>:   Charitable ☐   Personal ☐   Family ☐

Contact details of who is responsible for administering the Trust:

Name: ________________________________ Phone: ________________________________

Company: ____

<u>**LOCATION OF PERSONAL DOCUMENTS:**</u>

My personal documents *(e.g. relating to bank/financial, property, policies, personal identification, tax returns, copy of Will, etc)* as detailed in this booklet are located:

____

____

____

____

<u>**IMMEDIATE FAMILY MEMBERS:**</u> *(parent / daughter / son / sister / brother / stepchild / relative)*

<u>**SURNAME**</u>: _________________________________ **Given names**: _______________________________

Relationship to you: ____

Country of residence: _____________________________________ Phone: ______________________________

Email address: ____

<u>**SURNAME**</u>: _________________________________ **Given names**: _______________________________

Relationship to you: ____

Country of residence: _____________________________________ Phone: ______________________________

Email address: ____

<u>**SURNAME**</u>: _________________________________ **Given names**: _______________________________

Relationship to you: ____

Country of residence: _____________________________________ Phone: ______________________________

Email address: ____

<u>**SURNAME**</u>: _________________________________ **Given names**: _______________________________

Relationship to you: ____

Country of residence: _____________________________________ Phone: ______________________________

Email address: ____

<u>**SURNAME**</u>: _________________________________ **Given names**: _______________________________

Relationship to you: ____

Country of residence: _____________________________________ Phone: ______________________________

Email address: ____

<u>**SURNAME**</u>: _________________________________ **Given names**: _______________________________

Relationship to you: ____

Country of residence: _____________________________________ Phone: ______________________________

Email address: ____

<u>**SURNAME**</u>: _________________________________ **Given names**: _______________________________

Relationship to you: ____

Country of residence: _____________________________________ Phone: ______________________________

Email address: ____

IMMEDIATE FAMILY MEMBERS: *(parent / daughter / son / sister / brother / stepchild / relative)*

SURNAME: ________________________________ **Given names:** ________________________________

Relationship to you: ____

Country of residence: _________________________________ Phone: ________________________

Email address: ____

SURNAME: ________________________________ **Given names:** ________________________________

Relationship to you: ____

Country of residence: _________________________________ Phone: ________________________

Email address: ____

SURNAME: ________________________________ **Given names:** ________________________________

Relationship to you: ____

Country of residence: _________________________________ Phone: ________________________

Email address: ____

SURNAME: ________________________________ **Given names:** ________________________________

Relationship to you: ____

Country of residence: _________________________________ Phone: ________________________

Email address: ____

SURNAME: ________________________________ **Given names:** ________________________________

Relationship to you: ____

Country of residence: _________________________________ Phone: ________________________

Email address: ____

PETS:
Type of pet: ______________________________ Given Name: ________________________________

Type of pet: ______________________________ Given Name: ________________________________

Type of pet: ______________________________ Given Name: ________________________________

Type of pet: ______________________________ Given Name: ________________________________

PET/S HEALTH CARE: *(where your pet's vaccination and treatment history is recorded)*

Name of Vet: ______________________________ Clinic Name: ________________________________

Address: ____ Phone: ________________________

Name of Vet: ______________________________ Clinic Name: ________________________________

Address: ____ Phone: ________________________

NOTIFICATION: Individuals to be notified in the event of my death

Employer's name *(if applicable)*: _______________________________________

Phone: _________________________________ Email: _______________________________

Landlord's name or agency *(e.g. Real estate agent)*: _______________________

Phone: _________________________________ Email: _______________________________

____

Name: _______________________________ Country of residence: ________________

Phone: _________________________________ Email: _______________________________

Name: _______________________________ Country of residence: ________________

Phone: _________________________________ Email: _______________________________

Name: _______________________________ Country of residence: ________________

Phone: _________________________________ Email: _______________________________

Name: _______________________________ Country of residence: ________________

Phone: _________________________________ Email: _______________________________

Name: _______________________________ Country of residence: ________________

Phone: _________________________________ Email: _______________________________

Name: _______________________________ Country of residence: ________________

Phone: _________________________________ Email: _______________________________

Name: _______________________________ Country of residence: ________________

Phone: _________________________________ Email: _______________________________

Name: _______________________________ Country of residence: ________________

Phone: _________________________________ Email: _______________________________

Name: _______________________________ Country of residence: ________________

Phone: _________________________________ Email: _______________________________

Name: _______________________________ Country of residence: ________________

Phone: _________________________________ Email: _______________________________

<u>**Individuals to be notified in the event of my death:**</u>

Name: _______________________________ Country of residence: _______________________________

Phone: _______________________________ Email: _______________________________

Name: _______________________________ Country of residence: _______________________________

Phone: _______________________________ Email: _______________________________

Name: _______________________________ Country of residence: _______________________________

Phone: _______________________________ Email: _______________________________

Name: _______________________________ Country of residence: _______________________________

Phone: _______________________________ Email: _______________________________

Name: _______________________________ Country of residence: _______________________________

Phone: _______________________________ Email: _______________________________

Name: _______________________________ Country of residence: _______________________________

Phone: _______________________________ Email: _______________________________

Name: _______________________________ Country of residence: _______________________________

Phone: _______________________________ Email: _______________________________

Name: _______________________________ Country of residence: _______________________________

Phone: _______________________________ Email: _______________________________

Name: _______________________________ Country of residence: _______________________________

Phone: _______________________________ Email: _______________________________

Name: _______________________________ Country of residence: _______________________________

Phone: _______________________________ Email: _______________________________

Name: _______________________________ Country of residence: _______________________________

Phone: _______________________________ Email: _______________________________

Name: _______________________________ Country of residence: _______________________________

Phone: _______________________________ Email: _______________________________

Name: _______________________________ Country of residence: _______________________________

Phone: _______________________________ Email: _______________________________

Name: _______________________________ Country of residence: _______________________________

Phone: _______________________________ Email: _______________________________

<u>**Individuals to be notified in the event of my death:**</u>

<u>Name:</u> ________________________________ Country of residence: ________________________________

Phone: ________________________________ Email: ________________________________

<u>Name:</u> ________________________________ Country of residence: ________________________________

Phone: ________________________________ Email: ________________________________

<u>Name:</u> ________________________________ Country of residence: ________________________________

Phone: ________________________________ Email: ________________________________

<u>Name:</u> ________________________________ Country of residence: ________________________________

Phone: ________________________________ Email: ________________________________

<u>Name:</u> ________________________________ Country of residence: ________________________________

Phone: ________________________________ Email: ________________________________

<u>Name:</u> ________________________________ Country of residence: ________________________________

Phone: ________________________________ Email: ________________________________

<u>Name:</u> ________________________________ Country of residence: ________________________________

Phone: ________________________________ Email: ________________________________

<u>Name:</u> ________________________________ Country of residence: ________________________________

Phone: ________________________________ Email: ________________________________

<u>Name:</u> ________________________________ Country of residence: ________________________________

Phone: ________________________________ Email: ________________________________

<u>Name:</u> ________________________________ Country of residence: ________________________________

Phone: ________________________________ Email: ________________________________

<u>Name:</u> ________________________________ Country of residence: ________________________________

Phone: ________________________________ Email: ________________________________

<u>Name:</u> ________________________________ Country of residence: ________________________________

Phone: ________________________________ Email: ________________________________

<u>Name:</u> ________________________________ Country of residence: ________________________________

Phone: ________________________________ Email: ________________________________

<u>**Individuals to be notified in the event of my death:**</u>

Name: ______________________________   Country of residence: ______________________________

Phone: ______________________________   Email: ______________________________

Name: ______________________________   Country of residence: ______________________________

Phone: ______________________________   Email: ______________________________

Name: ______________________________   Country of residence: ______________________________

Phone: ______________________________   Email: ______________________________

Name: ______________________________   Country of residence: ______________________________

Phone: ______________________________   Email: ______________________________

Name: ______________________________   Country of residence: ______________________________

Phone: ______________________________   Email: ______________________________

Name: ______________________________   Country of residence: ______________________________

Phone: ______________________________   Email: ______________________________

Name: ______________________________   Country of residence: ______________________________

Phone: ______________________________   Email: ______________________________

Name: ______________________________   Country of residence: ______________________________

Phone: ______________________________   Email: ______________________________

Name: ______________________________   Country of residence: ______________________________

Phone: ______________________________   Email: ______________________________

Name: ______________________________   Country of residence: ______________________________

Phone: ______________________________   Email: ______________________________

Name: ______________________________   Country of residence: ______________________________

Phone: ______________________________   Email: ______________________________

Name: ______________________________   Country of residence: ______________________________

Phone: ______________________________   Email: ______________________________

Name: ______________________________   Country of residence: ______________________________

Phone: ______________________________   Email: ______________________________

Name: ______________________________   Country of residence: ______________________________

Phone: ______________________________   Email: ______________________________

FUNERAL

I have a Funeral Fund or Prepaid Funeral Plan: Yes ☐   No ☐

If 'Yes', my Funeral Plan / Fund is currently held with: Funeral Company ☐ Other ☐

Name of organisation / Contact person: ______________________________

Location/Address: _________________________________ **Phone:** _______________

DISPOSAL OF BODY - **The following are my wishes for the disposal of my body:**

I have specific cultural beliefs *(refer page 17)* ☐

I have discussed my wishes with the following person/s who has/have agreed to make decisions regarding my funeral and the disposal of my body. *(Be mindful that legally your appointed Executor will decide):*

Name: _________________________________ **Phone:** _______________

Name: _________________________________ **Phone:** _______________

EMBALMING: I do <u>NOT</u> wish to be embalmed ☐ but prefer that my body be disposed of as per my following preference, as soon as practicable, followed by a memorial service *(body not present).*

BURIAL: I wish to be buried ☐ at the following cemetery / burial ground / next to relatives etc:

____

____

I have purchased a burial plot, located at: _______________________________

I have no burial site preference ☐

I would like the following epitaph at my burial site: _______________________

____

CREMATION: I wish to be cremated ☐ and my ashes stored at *(e.g. name and address of crematorium):*

____

____

I prefer my ashes to be scattered as follows. *(Please consider impact on environment and/or cultural values and practices, as outlined on page 17):*

____

____

Other requests:

____

____

____

____

DEATH NOTICE / FUNERAL/MEMORIAL SERVICE

DEATH NOTICE: *Any requests regarding wording of Death Notice, e.g. In lieu of flowers, donations should be made to (name of organisation) etc:*

____

____

____

____

I would like my funeral/memorial service to be held at *(location e.g. of church, hall etc):*

____

____

Or: I have no preference for my funeral/memorial service location ☐

FUNERAL DIRECTOR/CELEBRANT: *(Provide contact details if you have a preference for any particular Funeral Director/Celebrant, Minister, friend who you wish to lead the funeral/memorial service)*

Name of Funeral Director: _______________________________ Phone: _______________________

Other: _______________________________ *(Celebrant/Minister/friend)* Phone: _______________________

TYPE OF SERVICE:

I would prefer a funeral service ☐ *(body present)* **Or** memorial service ☐ *(body NOT present)*

FLOWERS: I do NOT want flowers ☐   **Or:**   I want flowers ☐   and the flowers I prefer are:

____

RELIGION / FAITH: ____________________ **Or:**   Non denominational ☐

Or: I have specific cultural traditions or beliefs *(as described on page 17)* ☐

CASKET / COFFIN: *(Preferred type)*

I have no casket/coffin preference ☐   **Or:** The following is my casket/coffin preference:

____

I have purchased or made my casket ☐   Location: ___________________________________

At my funeral service I prefer that my casket is: OPEN ☐ CLOSED ☐

I would prefer viewing of my casket to be private, by family, close friends and relatives only ☐

PALLBEARERS of Casket/Coffin *(Names and contact details of preferred pallbearers):*

Name: _______________________________ Phone: _______________________

Name: _______________________________ Phone: _______________________

Name: _______________________________ Phone: _______________________

Name: _______________________________ Phone: _______________________

Name: _______________________________ Phone: _______________________

Name: _______________________________ Phone: _______________________

Name: _______________________________ Phone: _______________________

<u>**FUNERAL / MEMORIAL SERVICE FORMAT**</u>

I have no preference as to the format of my funeral/memorial service ☐

I am happy for family and friends to speak at my funeral/memorial service, if they wish ☐

I would like the following person/s to speak, or sing / play music at my funeral/memorial service:

Name: _______________________________________ Phone: ____________________

Name: _______________________________________ Phone: ____________________

Name: _______________________________________ Phone: ____________________

Name: _______________________________________ Phone: ____________________

MUSIC: I would like the following songs, hymns or music to be played at my funeral/memorial service. *(Indicate if you have a preference for when played, e.g. at beginning, during or at end of service)*:

<u>Title:</u>   ____

<u>Artist/Composer:</u> ____

<u>When played:</u> ____

<u>Title:</u>   ____

<u>Artist/Composer:</u> ____

<u>When played:</u> ____

<u>Title:</u>   ____

<u>Artist/Composer:</u> ____

<u>When played:</u> ____

<u>Title:</u>   ____

<u>Artist/Composer:</u> ____

<u>When played:</u> ____

POEMS / QUOTES: I would like the following poems or quotes to be read.
(Indicate if you have a preference for when read, e.g. at beginning, during or at end of service):

Title: ____________________________________ Written by ____________________

Title: ____________________________________ Written by ____________________

Title: ____________________________________ Written by ____________________

Title: ____________________________________ Written by ____________________

____

____

____

<u>**MESSAGES:**</u> I would like the following to be read or conveyed to individuals, family members, friends:

For: _______________________________ *(name)* To be read at my service ☐ To be read privately ☐

____

____

____

For: _______________________________ *(name)* To be read at my service ☐ To be read privately ☐

____

____

____

For: _______________________________ *(name)* To be read at my service ☐ To be read privately ☐

____

____

____

For: _______________________________ *(name)* To be read at my service ☐ To be read privately ☐

____

____

____

Any other funeral requests or preferences *(e.g. for order of service)*:

____

____

I am happy for personal photos/videos to be displayed or shown: Yes ☐   No ☐

Location of my personal photos or videos *(if with family member/friend, provide name, contact details)*:

____

<u>**CULTURAL BELIEFS / TRADITIONS**</u>

You may have religious or cultural beliefs, specific traditions or ceremonies that you wish to be observed regarding the disposal of your body and/or the type and format of your funeral. Record these here. Your Executor should also be made aware of these, if you have appointed one (refer to page 5).

Please contact the following person, who is aware of my cultural traditions:

Name: ____ **Phone:** ___________________________________

____

____

____

____

____

____

____

____

____

____

____

____

____

____

____

____

____

____

____

____

____

____

____

MY LIFE STORY

(To assist speaker/s at your funeral/memorial service in outlining your life story, e.g. where you lived, schools attended, study, career, employment, military service (where served, war, rank, Unit/Regiment, any medals awarded), family, travel, achievements/awards, skills/hobbies, humorous and other significant events).

PERSONAL IDENTIFICATION

Passport number: _______________________ Citizenship/resident of: _______________________

Drivers licence number: _______________________ Country: _______________________

Tax file number: _______________________ Country: _______________________

Social security / welfare benefit number: _______________________

CITIZENSHIP: I am also a citizen of these countries:

Passport number: _______________________ Citizen/resident of: _______________________

Drivers licence number: _______________________ Tax file number: _______________________

Most recent address in this country: _______________________

Passport number: _______________________ Citizen/resident of: _______________________

Drivers licence number: _______________________ Tax file number: _______________________

Most recent address in this country: _______________________

PERSONAL PRIVATE POST OFFICE BOX:

I have a Post Office box: ☐ Location: _______________________

SAFE DEPOSIT BOX:

I have a safe deposit box: ☐ Location: _______________________

(Either keep the key with your documents) <u>or</u> Contact: _______________________

SERVICE PROVIDERS:

Property location (main residence): _______________________

Electricity supplier: _______________________ Account no: _______________________

Landline/internet/broadband: _______________________ Account no: _______________________

Mobile phone provider: _______________________

Service Providers at other properties owned / rented:

Property location: _______________________

Electricity supplier: _______________________ Account no: _______________________

Landline/internet/broadband: _______________________ Account no: _______________________

Property location: _______________________

Electricity supplier: _______________________ Account no: _______________________

Landline/internet/broadband: _______________________ Account no: _______________________

Other: _______________________

FINANCE

Name of Financial Adviser: _________________________________ **Phone:** ________________

Organisation / Address: ____

Name of Accountant: _____________________________________ **Phone:** ________________

Organisation / Address: ____

BANK ACCOUNT/S and TYPE *(e.g. savings/cheque/credit card/term deposit)*:

- **Bank:** ____ **Branch:** ________________

  Account name: _______________________________ **Or** this is a joint account ☐ with:

  (Name/contact details): ____

  Account type: ____

- **Bank:** ____ **Branch:** ________________

  Account name: _______________________________ **Or** this is a joint account ☐ with:

  (Name/contact details): ____

  Account type: ____

- **Bank:** ____ **Branch:** ________________

  Account name: _______________________________ **Or** this is a joint account ☐ with:

  (Name/contact details): ____

  Account type: ____

- **Bank:** ____ **Branch:** ________________

  Account name: _______________________________ **Or** this is a joint account ☐ with:

  (Name/contact details): ____

  Account type: ____

- **Bank:** ____ **Branch:** ________________

  Account name: _______________________________ **Or** this is a joint account ☐ with:

  (Name/contact details): ____

  Account type: ____

OTHER SAVINGS ACCOUNTS

Account held with *(name of organisation):* _____________________________________

Phone: _______________________ Address: ___________________________________

Account held with *(name of organisation):* _____________________________________

Phone: _______________________ Address: ___________________________________

RETIREMENT INCOME *(e.g. Superannuation, pension etc)*

I have a retirement income plan / fund with: ____

Policy No: ____ Phone: _______________________

Address: ____

This plan / fund includes Death Cover: Yes ☐ No ☐

____

I have another retirement income plan/fund (e.g. in another country) with: _______________________

Policy No: ____ Phone: _______________________

Address ____

This plan / fund includes Death Cover: Yes ☐ No ☐

____

INVESTMENTS:

Name (Investment broker): _________________________________ Phone: ________________________

Address: ____

SHARES:

Name (Share broker): _________________________________ Phone: ________________________

Address: ____

I have shares and/or other investments held with:

Name of company: ____

Phone: ______________________________ Address: ___________________________________

Name of company: ____

Phone: ______________________________ Address: ___________________________________

Name of company: ____

Phone: ______________________________ Address: ___________________________________

Name of company: ____

Phone: ______________________________ Address: ___________________________________

OTHER INCOME:

I receive regular income from, e.g. rental property, business etc *(see pages 24/25)* ☐ Other ☐

<u>Details</u>: *(if property, provide address, contact details of tenant, etc)*

____

____

____

<u>**BUSINESS OWNERSHIP:**</u> *(If you operate your own business or with a partner/s, provide details)*

BUSINESS 1: Name of business: ____

Jointly with: ____

Type of business: ____

Who to consult: ____________________________________ Phone: _______________________

BUSINESS 2: Name of business: ____

Jointly with: ____

Type of business: ____

Who to consult: ____________________________________ Phone: _______________________

BUSINESS 3: Name of business: ____

Jointly with: ____

Type of business: ____

Who to consult: ____________________________________ Phone: _______________________

<u>**Other:**</u>

____

____

____

____

____

____

<u>**PROPERTY / PROPERTIES OWNED:**</u>

I own a property located at: ____

with ownership title in my name alone ☐ <u>or</u> jointly ☐ with: ___________________________

(If jointly, provide contact details): ____

There is a mortgage on this property: No ☐ <u>or</u> Yes ☐ held with: ______________________

                (e.g. name of bank)

____

My Lawyer has details of the property I / We own ☐
(If not held with Lawyer, provide details regarding location of any other property /properties owned):

____

____

____

This property is currently rented to: ____________________________ Phone: ______________

I own a property located at: ____

with ownership title in my name alone ☐ <u>or</u> jointly ☐ with: ______________________

(If jointly, provide contact details): ____

There is a mortgage on this property: No ☐ <u>or</u> Yes ☐ held with: __________________

(e.g. name of bank)

____

My Lawyer has details of the property I / We own ☐

(If not held with Lawyer, provide details regarding location of any other property /properties owned):

____

____

This property is currently rented to: ______________________ Phone: ______________

I own a property located at: ____

with ownership title in my name alone ☐ <u>or</u> jointly ☐ with: ______________________

(If jointly, provide contact details): ____

There is a mortgage on this property: No ☐ <u>or</u> Yes ☐ held with: __________________

(e.g. name of bank)

____

My Lawyer has details of the property I / We own ☐

(If not held with Lawyer, provide details regarding location of any other property /properties owned):

____

____

This property is currently rented to: ______________________ Phone: ______________

I own a property located at: ____

with ownership title in my name alone ☐ <u>or</u> jointly ☐ with: ______________________

(If jointly, provide contact details): ____

There is a mortgage on this property: No ☐ <u>or</u> Yes ☐ held with: __________________

(e.g. name of bank)

____

My Lawyer has details of the property I / We own ☐

(If not held with Lawyer, provide details regarding location of any other property /properties owned):

____

____

This property is currently rented to: ______________________ Phone: ______________

<u>**REGULAR PAYMENTS:**</u> *(e.g. rent, donations, loan repayments, e.g. mortgage, motor vehicle loan)*

From my _______________________________________ **to** _______________________________________
(name of bank account)   *(name of company/individual)*

I make the following regular payment of $ __________   for __________________________ *(e.g. rent)*

Weekly ☐   Fortnightly ☐   Monthly ☐   Other ☐ __________________ *(frequency)*

From my _______________________________________ **to** _______________________________________
(name of bank account)   *(name of company/individual)*

I make the following regular payment of $ __________   for __________________________ *(e.g. rent)*

Weekly ☐   Fortnightly ☐   Monthly ☐   Other ☐ __________________ *(frequency)*

From my _______________________________________ **to** _______________________________________
(name of bank account)   *(name of company/individual)*

I make the following regular payment of $ __________   for __________________________ *(e.g. rent)*

Weekly ☐   Fortnightly ☐   Monthly ☐   Other ☐ __________________ *(frequency)*

From my _______________________________________ **to** _______________________________________
(name of bank account)   *(name of company/individual)*

I make the following regular payment of $ __________   for __________________________ *(e.g. rent)*

Weekly ☐   Fortnightly ☐   Monthly ☐   Other ☐ __________________ *(frequency)*

From my _______________________________________ **to** _______________________________________
(name of bank account)   *(name of company/individual)*

I make the following regular payment of $ __________   for __________________________ *(e.g. rent)*

Weekly ☐   Fortnightly ☐   Monthly ☐   Other ☐ __________________ *(frequency)*

From my _______________________________________ **to** _______________________________________
(name of bank account)   *(name of company/individual)*

I make the following regular payment of $ __________   for __________________________ *(e.g. rent)*

Weekly ☐   Fortnightly ☐   Monthly ☐   Other ☐ __________________ *(frequency)*

<u>**PERSONAL DEBTS**</u>   *(e.g. to or from someone):*

I currently <u>owe</u> $ __________   to ___________________________________ Phone: _______________

I currently <u>owe</u> $ __________   to ___________________________________ Phone: _______________

I currently <u>owe</u> $ __________   to ___________________________________ Phone: _______________

I am currently <u>owed</u> $ __________   by ___________________________________ Phone: _______________

I am currently <u>owed</u> $ __________   by ___________________________________ Phone: _______________

I am currently <u>owed</u> $ __________   by ___________________________________ Phone: _______________

MEMBERSHIPS / SUBSCRIPTIONS

I am a member of the following organisations:

Name of organisation: ________________________________ Membership No: ________________

Phone: ____________________ Address: ____

Name of organisation: ________________________________ Membership No: ________________

Phone: ____________________ Address: ____

Name of organisation: ________________________________ Membership No: ________________

Phone: ____________________ Address: ____

Name of organisation: ________________________________ Membership No: ________________

Phone: ____________________ Address: ____

Name of organisation: ________________________________ Membership No: ________________

Phone: ____________________ Address: ____

Name of organisation: ________________________________ Membership No: ________________

Phone: ____________________ Address: ____

Name of organisation: ________________________________ Membership No: ________________

Phone: ____________________ Address: ____

Name of organisation: ________________________________ Membership No: ________________

Phone: ____________________ Address: ____

SUBSCRIPTIONS: *(List name of magazine, newspaper etc)*

I subscribe to: __________________________ **Supplier:** __________________________

I subscribe to: __________________________ **Supplier:** __________________________

I subscribe to: __________________________ **Supplier:** __________________________

I subscribe to: __________________________ **Supplier:** __________________________

I subscribe to: __________________________ **Supplier:** __________________________

I subscribe to: __________________________ **Supplier:** __________________________

INSURANCE/S

LIFE INSURANCE: I do <u>NOT</u> have a Life Insurance policy ☐   **<u>Or</u>: I have a Life Insurance policy with:**

Name of insurance company: _______________________________   Phone: _______________________

Address: ____

Policy No: _____________________________________   **Is this policy jointly owned?   No** ☐   **Yes** ☐

If 'Yes', with who?   Name: _______________________________   Phone: _______________________

<u>Or</u>: I have life insurance on the following person's *(e.g. spouse)* **life:**

Name *(e.g. of spouse)*: _______________________________   Phone: _______________________

Name and address of insurance company: ____

____   Policy no: _______________________

OTHER INSURANCE POLICIES *(e.g. Health, Property, Motor vehicle etc)*:

Name of insurance company: _______________________________   Phone: _______________________

Address: ____

Type of insurance cover: _______________________________   Policy no: _______________________

Name of insurance company: _______________________________   Phone: _______________________

Address: ____

Type of insurance cover: _______________________________   Policy no: _______________________

Name of insurance company: _______________________________   Phone: _______________________

Address: ____

Type of insurance cover: _______________________________   Policy no: _______________________

Name of insurance company: _______________________________   Phone: _______________________

Address: ____

Type of insurance cover: _______________________________   Policy no: _______________________

Name of insurance company: _______________________________   Phone: _______________________

Address: ____

Type of insurance cover: _______________________________   Policy no: _______________________

Name of insurance company: _______________________________   Phone: _______________________

Address: ____

Type of insurance cover: _______________________________   Policy no: _______________________

HEALTH

Personal professionals to be notified in the event of my death:

DENTIST: ____   Phone: ___________________

DOCTOR: ____   Phone: ___________________

MEDICAL PRACTICE: ___________________________________   Phone: ___________________

Other therapists: ___________________________________   Phone: ___________________

____   Phone: ___________________

Health care service number: ___________________________________

Medical Record Number (your hospital identification number): ___________________________

HEALTH INSURANCE: Name of insurance company: ____

Phone: ___________________   Address: ____

Type of health cover: ___________________________________   Policy no: ___________________

ORGAN and TISSUE DONATION *(Please discuss with your family, who may be asked to make this decision):*

I do **NOT** wish to donate organs / tissues for transplants ☐

I do **NOT** want my body to be used for medical research ☐

Or: I wish to donate these organs / tissues for transplants:

Heart ☐   Pancreas ☐   Kidneys ☐   Liver ☐   Lungs ☐   Intestine ☐

Skin ☐   Eye tissue ☐   Ligaments ☐   Tendons ☐   Bone ☐   Heart valves/ Tissue ☐

This request has been recorded on my Drivers Licence: Yes ☐   No ☐

I have discussed my organ / tissue donation with my family: Yes ☐   No ☐

I would like my body and/or organs to be donated for medical research, as follows:

____

MEDICAL CARE: *(if you are incapacitated and/or unable to advise your wishes)*

I have completed an Advance Care Plan *(refer to page 6)*   ☐

I wish to be kept alive in hospital on life support if recovery is unlikely: Yes ☐   No ☐

I agree to blood transfusions and/or medication in order to sustain my life: Yes ☐   No ☐

Specific requests:

____

I have advised the following person/s of these requests: *(Provide name and contact details, or if you have a nominated Power of Attorney refer to page 6):*

Name/s: ___________________________________   Phone: ___________________

Name/s: ___________________________________   Phone: ___________________

DISTRIBUTION OF PERSONAL ITEMS / GIFTS

These items may be small gifts to family members, heirlooms, items that have sentimental value or no value at all, but you would like to give them to someone in particular. Be mindful however that whatever you have specified in your Will overrides what you list below and that unless a gift is recorded in your Will, that item may form part of the residue of your estate and go to whoever you have nominated to receive this.

I do NOT have a Will ☐   My Will refers to this distribution list ☐

My lawyer holds a copy of this list ☐   My lawyer is NOT aware of this list ☐

<u>DISTRIBUTION:</u>

I would like my personal items to be distributed as follows:

Gift to: _______________________________   **Item:** _______________________________

Location: ____

History of item/how acquired *(e.g. grandmother's ring)*:

____

Gift to: _______________________________   **Item:** _______________________________

Location: ____

History of item/how acquired:

____

Gift to: _______________________________   **Item:** _______________________________

Location: ____

History of item/how acquired:

____

Gift to: _______________________________   **Item:** _______________________________

Location: ____

History of item/how acquired:

____

Gift to: _______________________________   **Item:** _______________________________

Location: ____

History of item/how acquired:

____

Gift to: ________________________________   Item: ______________________________________

Location: ____

History of item/how acquired:

____

Gift to: ________________________________   Item: ______________________________________

Location: ____

History of item/how acquired:

____

Gift to: ________________________________   Item: ______________________________________

Location: ____

History of item/how acquired:

____

Gift to: ________________________________   Item: ______________________________________

Location: ____

History of item/how acquired:

____

Gift to: ________________________________   Item: ______________________________________

Location: ____

History of item/how acquired:

____

Gift to: ________________________________   Item: ______________________________________

Location: ____

History of item/how acquired:

____

Gift to: ________________________________   Item: ______________________________________

Location: ____

History of item/how acquired:

____

Gift to: ________________________________   Item: ______________________________________

Location: ____

History of item/how acquired:

____

Gift to: _________________________________   Item: _______________________________________

Location: ____

History of item/how acquired:

____

Gift to: _________________________________   Item: _______________________________________

Location: ____

History of item/how acquired:

____

Gift to: _________________________________   Item: _______________________________________

Location: ____

History of item/how acquired:

____

Gift to: _________________________________   Item: _______________________________________

Location: ____

History of item/how acquired:

____

Gift to: _________________________________   Item: _______________________________________

Location: ____

History of item/how acquired:

____

Gift to: _________________________________   Item: _______________________________________

Location: ____

History of item/how acquired:

____

Gift to: _________________________________   Item: _______________________________________

Location: ____

History of item/how acquired:

____

Gift to: _________________________________   Item: _______________________________________

Location: ____

History of item/how acquired:

____

Gift to: _________________________________   **Item:** _________________________________

Location: ____

History of item/how acquired:

____

Gift to: _________________________________   **Item:** _________________________________

Location: ____

History of item/how acquired:

____

Gift to: _________________________________   **Item:** _________________________________

Location: ____

History of item/how acquired:

____

Gift to: _________________________________   **Item:** _________________________________

Location: ____

History of item/how acquired:

____

Gift to: _________________________________   **Item:** _________________________________

Location: ____

History of item/how acquired:

____

Gift to: _________________________________   **Item:** _________________________________

Location: ____

History of item/how acquired:

____

Gift to: _________________________________   **Item:** _________________________________

Location: ____

History of item/how acquired:

____

Gift to: _________________________________   **Item:** _________________________________

Location: ____

History of item/how acquired:

____

Gift to: ______________________________   **Item:** ______________________________

Location: ____

History of item/how acquired:

____

Gift to: ______________________________   **Item:** ______________________________

Location: ____

History of item/how acquired:

____

Gift to: ______________________________   **Item:** ______________________________

Location: ____

History of item/how acquired:

____

Gift to: ______________________________   **Item:** ______________________________

Location: ____

History of item/how acquired:

____

Gift to: ______________________________   **Item:** ______________________________

Location: ____

History of item/how acquired:

____

Gift to: ______________________________   **Item:** ______________________________

Location: ____

History of item/how acquired:

____

Gift to: ______________________________   **Item:** ______________________________

Location: ____

History of item/how acquired:

____

Gift to: ______________________________   **Item:** ______________________________

Location: ____

History of item/how acquired: ____

COMPUTER / TECHNOLOGY ACCESS / EMAIL ACCOUNTS

Have you considered giving password/access details for your technology (e.g. iPad/tablet, mobile phone, computer) to at least two trusted friends or family members? Alternatively, let them know where this information is stored.

Remember to include the access details for your social media, on-line registrations and memberships which will need to be unsubscribed / cancelled, e.g. eBay, Facebook, Trip Advisor, Airbnb, Dropbox, LinkedIn, Frequent Flyer/Airpoints etc.

For the purpose of accessing my computer/technology in order to cancel my social media or other memberships in the event of my death, I have advised the following person/s regarding my access details/ password/s and their whereabouts:

Contact details:

Name: _______________________________   Phone: _______________________________

Name: _______________________________   Phone: _______________________________

Name: _______________________________   Phone: _______________________________

Name: _______________________________   Phone: _______________________________

EMAILS: My personal email address/es are:

_______________________________   _______________________________

_______________________________   _______________________________

_______________________________   _______________________________

_______________________________   _______________________________

ONLINE REGISTRATIONS / MEMBERSHIPS:

I have a Facebook account ☐   I do **NOT** have a Facebook account ☐

List other social media, on-line registrations and/or memberships which should be cancelled or unsubscribed, *e.g. eBay, Trip Advisor, Airbnb, Dropbox, LinkedIn, Frequent Flyer/Airpoints etc:*

_______________________________   _______________________________

_______________________________   _______________________________

_______________________________   _______________________________

_______________________________   _______________________________

_______________________________   _______________________________

_______________________________   _______________________________

BORROWED / LOANED ITEMS

Items that I have <u>borrowed from others</u> which are in my possession, and should be returned:

Item: ____

Borrowed from: ____

Contact details: ____

Item: ____

Borrowed from: ____

Contact details: ____

Item: ____

Borrowed from: ____

Contact details: ____

Item: ____

Borrowed from: ____

Contact details: ____

Item: ____

Borrowed from: ____

Contact details: ____

Items that I have <u>loaned to others</u> which should be returned to my family / estate:

Item: ____

Loaned to: ____

Contact details: ____

Item: ____

Loaned to: ____

Contact details: ____

Item: ____

Loaned to: ____

Contact details: ____

Item: ____

Loaned to: ____

Contact details: ____

AMENDMENTS

Record any changes that have been made since your original completion of this booklet. You may wish to change your original request, or record a change of name, e.g. if an organisation has changed its name, address or phone number, or an individual's name has changed (as a result of marriage) etc. Where changes apply within the booklet, you may wish to write 'see amendment' (against the entry) and itemise these here:

Change as recorded on page no: ______

Original request: ____

New request: ____

Change as recorded on page no: ______

Original request: ____

New request: ____

Change as recorded on page no: ______

Original request: ____

New request: ____

Change as recorded on page no: ______

Original request: ____

New request: ____

Change as recorded on page no: ______

Original request: ____

New request: ____

Change as recorded on page no: ______

Original request: ____

New request: ____

Change as recorded on page no: ______

Original request: ____

New request: ____

Change as recorded on page no: ______

Original request: ____

New request: ____

Change as recorded on page no: ______

Original request: ____

New request: ____

Change as recorded on page no: _______

Original request: ____

New request: ____

Change as recorded on page no: _______

Original request: ____

New request: ____

Change as recorded on page no: _______

Original request: ____

New request: ____

Change as recorded on page no: _______

Original request: ____

New request: ____

Change as recorded on page no: _______

Original request: ____

New request: ____

NAME CHANGES:

Change of name as recorded on page no: _______

Original request: ____

New request: ____

Change of name as recorded on page no: _______

Original request: ____

New request: ____

Change of name as recorded on page no: _______

Original request: ____

New request: ____

Change of name as recorded on page no: _______

Original request: ____

New request: ____

Change of name as recorded on page no: _______

Original request: ____

New request: ____

OTHER INFORMATION / REQUESTS

OTHER INFORMATION / REQUESTS

www.ingramcontent.com/pod-product-compliance
Lightning Source LLC
Chambersburg PA
CBHW080506030726
47592CB00011B/3267